Story of a Priest

Dialogue, Closeness and Communion

Lazarus You Heung-sik

Foreword by
Pope Francis

An Interview by
Francesco Cosentino

NCP
NEW CITY PRESS

Published in the United States by New City Press
136 Madison Avenue, Floors 5 & 6, PMB #4290
New York, NY 10016
www.newcitypress.com

© 2025 New City Press (English translation)

Translated from the Italian original edition
Come la folgore viene da Oriente
(Francesco Cosentino & Lazarus You Heung-sik)
by Maria Blanc.

Cover photo: Djcatholic
Back cover photo: Lorenzo Iorfino

Layout and design: Miguel Tejerina

ISBN: 978-1-56548-726-0 (Paperback)
ISBN: 978-1-56548-727-7 (E-book)

Library of Congress Control Number: 2025943366

Printed in the United States of America

Contents

Foreword

After waiting many years for the consolation of the Lord, the elderly Simeon recognizes in the Child the Messiah sent by God. He takes him in his arms and blesses God with a heart full of emotion, recognizing in that Child the light of salvation that all peoples were awaiting (cf. Lk 2:30-31).

Jesus is the light sent by the Father into the dark nights of humanity. He is the dawn that God wanted to bring forth while we were still walking in darkness. He is the one who opened paths of hope where we were lost, illuminating the remote corners of the earth and the furrows of our broken, afflicted, and wounded hearts. He is the original light of Creation that now shines among us to dispel the darkness in our lives. Jesus is the light of the world (cf. Jn 8:12) and, therefore, even if we sometimes grope in the dark and lack "vision," there is hope for us. For we can always go to him, crying out like blind Bartimaeus, and receive from Jesus new and luminous eyes.

Inspired by this hope, the Church, in her theological and liturgical tradition, has always looked to the East, and she invites us to look there because from the East comes the light, the sun of justice, the shining star that is Christ. The Church always needs to be enlightened by Christ and his Gospel because, like a boat traversing the often rough waves of history, it runs the risk of not being the Church of Jesus. The elderly Simeon says to Mary and Joseph that this Child who has been born "is destined for the fall and rise of many in Israel, and to be a sign that will be opposed" (Lk 2:34). Jesus continues to be a scandal even today, a sign of contradiction that challenges our certainties and shakes our hearts so that they are not paralyzed by fear, imprisoned by hypocrisy, or hardened by sin. For the joy of the Gospel, while it comforts and uplifts us, is also a prophecy that challenges us, that continues to disturb the logic of human power, worldly calculations, the weapons of oppression, the logic of division and ambiguity. Jesus continues to be the One who disturbs the false peace of those who "look beautiful on the outside, but on the inside they are full of the bones of the dead and all kinds of filth . . . full of hypocrisy and lawlessness" (Mt 23:27-28).

This is why I am pleased to present this book, which aims to give voice to the Church of the East through the stories, anecdotes, and reflections of Cardinal Lazarus You Heung-sik, whom I met for the first time in 2014, during Asian Youth Day, and whom I have now called to lead the Dicastery for the Clergy. With his amiable and affable manner, he allows us to reap the fruits of a faith sown in the land of martyrs and nurtured with simplicity through the joyful witness of a living Church. From the story that slowly takes shape, we can glimpse the path for all of us to remain a Church faithful to Jesus and his Gospel, far from all worldliness.

From the conversations reported in these pages, which intertwine autobiographical elements with spiritual and pastoral reflections, Cardinal Lazarus brings out the portrait of a faith born of constant contact with the Word of God and with witnesses to the Gospel; the portrait of a young and enterprising Church, born of the laity, which becomes an instrument of hope and compassion, caring for the wounded; the portrait of a priestly ministry that needs to be regenerated in the light of the Gospel, emptying itself of all clericalism and rethinking itself "close to" and "with" its lay brothers and sisters, in community—both synodal and ministerial.

I therefore express my gratitude to Cardinal Lazarus and to those who have edited these pages. For we all need this light that comes from the East. We need to listen to the courageous witness of so many sisters and brothers who, with enthusiasm and despite much suffering, have welcomed Jesus with open arms, as did the elderly Simeon, welcoming the preaching of Saint Andrew Kim and the many missionaries who have given their lives for the joy of the Gospel. We need to "decenter ourselves," journey to the East and place ourselves in the school of a spiritual and ecclesial way of life that can reinvigorate our faith. And we need to remember that even in our struggles and darkness, like a thunderbolt, the Lord comes. And he wants to illuminate our lives.

Vatican City, February 2, 2023
Feast of the Presentation of the Lord

Francesco

Introduction

During his visit to Korea for the sixth Asian Youth Day, which took place between August 13 and 18, 2014, Pope Francis wanted to emphasize that the Church in Asia, with its diversity and vastness, represents a constant frontier for the witness of the Gospel, which calls the entire Christian community to dialogue with everyone. But Francis also wanted to stress that "there can be no authentic dialogue unless we are able to open our minds and hearts, with empathy and sincere acceptance, toward those with whom we speak."

When you meet Cardinal Lazarus You Heung-sik, who has been called by the Holy Father to lead the Dicastery for the Clergy, you immediately get the feeling of being at home, of being welcomed in an "open space" that fosters genuinely human, sincere, and straightforward communication, unencumbered by formalities and pleasantries. The empathy Pope Francis spoke of during that trip to Korea, the fruit of a "spiritual gaze . . . that leads us to see others as brothers and sisters, to 'listen,' through and beyond their words and actions, to what their hearts desire to communicate," is what Don Lazarus—as he affably wishes to be called—conveys from the very beginning: with his simple and open smile, the trait of goodness that you glimpse when you meet his eyes, the affectionate cordiality with which he welcomes you.

In the atmosphere created by his warm simplicity, I began to talk with him by, first of all, listening to his personal and spiritual story, cherishing the time we shared, convinced that the perspective that comes from the East, from that young, vibrant Church, fertilized by the blood of the martyrs, comes "like lightning" (cf. Mt 24:27) and can help all of us shift our gaze, open our minds and hearts to read and interpret the challenges of the Church with the eyes of the periphery, to welcome with renewed enthusiasm the joy of the Gospel.

Francesco Cosentino

The Golden Thread
of a Simple Story

*E*ach of us is shaped by a life story that, even before we have achieved anything along the way, says something important about who we really are and about our characteristic traits. You were born at a difficult time for Korea, almost at the end of the war, in a context where Christians had been persecuted for a long time and the Christian faith had weakened. In many families, Christ was either unknown or met with indifference. Yet, the joy of the Gospel made its way and, over the years, attracted many people like you, who then responded to the Lord's call by choosing the path of

1

the priesthood. It is as if we find ourselves immersed in those biblical pages in which the prophets announce that, precisely in the very barrenness of the desert, the Lord opens a way, and that from a small shoot something good can grow, if we have the patience to walk, to cultivate the seed of the Gospel, and to guard it.

～

But who is Cardinal Lazarus really?

Once in Korea they chose one hundred people, referring to them as those who have contributed to changing the world, and I was among them with a likable description: "A friend of all, with his smile, he conquers people." This is the title they chose for me, not because I had done anything great to change the world, but perhaps because small acts, even a simple smile, can change lives when we know how to live and bring joy. In truth, when I think about my story, I always remember the first interview Pope Francis gave to *La Civiltà Cattolica* after being elected, in which he spoke of himself as a sinner to whom the Lord turned his gaze, choosing him, calling him, but above all, guiding him on his journey, even *through* his mistakes and falls.

That is exactly how I feel. I see that there is a golden thread, God's love, that has always accompanied me. When I have some time or can enjoy a small break, even if only for an hour, I always try to look at myself not with my own eyes but by practicing "seeing with the eyes of God." And then I receive a special grace: I see this golden thread in my life.

I was born during the war in Korea; there was my mom, sister, brother, and me, while I don't remember anything about my father. Someone told me years later that he may have gone to North Korea, but we don't know for sure. In fact, it is a little difficult to reconstruct the events of that historical moment, marked by so many ideological divisions between North and South and by the presence of communism. In any case, mine was a poor family. They said I was a simple boy, even a very joyful one, but there was one thing I often heard people say about me and regarding my character. They describe me as a decisive person who carries things through with determination. In fact, they used to say:

If he takes the right path, he will be great, but if he chooses the wrong one, he will be worse than others, the worst of all! This is an ironic way of saying that in terms of character, I live totally and to the fullest who I am, what I decide, or what I am entrusted with. In fact, already during elementary school, I was a small group leader.

Giving Life in Faithfulness

During my middle school years, I had to cover eight kilometers to school, which took over an hour because I had to walk. In winter, it was very cold and sometimes it rained; yet, I never missed a day of school. It's not a boast. That is just how I am. I do what I have to do, and I'm not conditioned by other people's opinions or by obstacles. With simplicity, I go forward. I can tell you another story, perhaps even more telling. When I was studying in Rome, my bishop had an audience with John Paul II and took me along as his secretary. When I greeted the Pope, I spontaneously said, "Holy Father, I am ready to give my life for you and for the Church." The Pope was pleased, asked me what I was studying, and then gave me a very big hug, giving me three rosaries instead of one! Four months later, a letter from the Pope was published inviting the priests of the diocese of Rome to wear ecclesiastical attire. That was a somewhat turbulent period. I remember meeting a German friend and walking around the Spanish Steps for an hour, and all our comments were negative. "How could the Pope have written this? Times have changed," and things like that. But after a while, I told him that only one thing resonated in my conscience. I had told the Pope that I was ready to give my life for him and for the Church, and now I was backing down because of an outfit?

Life is much more than an attire! So, we went to a store where they sold clergy shirts and bought some. Even now, when I write letters to the Pope, I repeat, "Holy Father, I am ready to give my life for you and for the Church." And even when I became a cardinal, I reaffirmed this, and Pope Francis told me, "Good, good. Keep going!"

That's a glimpse of my character. But all these anecdotes serve to highlight the "golden thread" I was mentioning. I feel and see how the Lord uses our character in his own way; he makes use of us as we are. For us, the issue is whether we use our lives to serve and love, or only for ourselves. We may be very intelligent, people of great ability, but the question remains the same: How do I use this [talent]? Therefore, just as back then with school, here in the Dicastery I try never to be absent, just as I remain faithful to my morning walk, during which I stop at the Grotto of the Virgin of Lourdes in the Vatican Gardens to pray, even if it rains, because after all, there are such things as umbrellas! Here, I see that the Lord has used this trait of mine, this way of mine of carrying things forward, and as I look back, I see this thread which he has worked precisely through the way I am made.

First Contact with the Catholic Church and Baptism

Let's return to the [topic of] school. In middle school, I attended a Catholic school named after Andrew Kim Taegon, who would later become so important in my life. This is where I first came into contact with the Catholic Church. In fact, no one in my family was a believer. That was a time when the Catholic Church was still very small. It had been persecuted in the past and, therefore, had become a Church somewhat concerned about "maintaining" the faith; that is, preserving doctrine. Proclaiming the Gospel was not something that excited a lot. Religion class was fundamental for me at school, during which I learned the history of the Old Testament and then the first things about Jesus. Then I went to high school. I had been recommended to attend the best high school in town, but my mother was worried because I would have to leave home, find a place to stay, and incur a cost that was not easy for people like us who were of modest means. So, I enrolled in another high school, also a Catholic school, named after Andrew Kim, where they also offered scholarships. Starting this new journey, with the open-mindedness it generated and the intellectual curiosity it aroused, I began to take an interest in those European and American countries that lived better than we did; some of these countries, many of which were Christian, had even helped us during the war. It seemed to me that it was their Christian spirit that had prompted them to come out, to meet our difficulties during the war, to live charity. And so I wanted to get to know them better and to deepen my understanding of Christian culture. Precisely because, as I said, when I start something or have a goal, I see it through, I enrolled in a special course offered by the school, where people were preparing to receive Baptism. I got along very well with the people who were taking this course and with those who were teaching catechism. In the end, on Christmas Eve 1966, at the age of sixteen, I willingly received the Sacrament of Baptism. Just as Pope Francis said when he came to Korea for Asian Youth Day, the Christian faith in Korea, through a mysterious and providential plan of God, came not through missionaries, but through the hearts and minds of the Korean people themselves, who were stimulated by intellectual curiosity, sought the truth, and wanted to know more about Jesus, his life, suffering, death, and resurrection. And this led us to a more personal encounter with him and to receive Baptism.

A Committed Young Man Inspired by Andrew Kim

No one, however, told me at first that it was important to go to Mass on Sundays. After a few months, the school decided to give me a scholarship, and I learned that the money came from some Catholic women in Austria. Once again, that unexpected gesture of charity surprised me, and the Lord was using it to draw me to himself. These women, who did not know me and were from another part of the world, had given me important help. I wanted to thank them but had no way to do so. So, I thought, they are Catholics, the only thing I can do is to go to church and pray for them. And, so, I started going to church. I had received something, and I felt the need to say thank you. My participation in the Eucharist, which is precisely an act of thanksgiving, was born in this way. This experience reinforced my belief that the Lord leads us, and his grace is always at work, not in extraordinary things, but when we say yes to small things and carry them out—the golden thread I mentioned before. From that moment on, I became a young man involved in the activities of the Church. At that time, a lay Catholic organization called *Legio Mariae* arrived in Korea. It had weekly meetings where we first recited the rosary, and then each person committed to a good deed to be done by the following week. Some of us often committed to cleaning the school bathrooms, which were very dirty. We did it willingly. In that humble service, we discovered the joy of being Christians. Above all, I learned one important thing: Christianity is concrete, not a theoretical idea. The Christian faith has to do with life, not theories.

Being concrete also means something else: The Christian faith opens people to life, to living life to the fullest. Let me explain with an example. I remember that there was a big competition, promoted by the diocese, to educate the faithful and spread the tenets of the faith. All of us kids committed ourselves to studying the catechism, which, back then, consisted of questions and answers. To prepare us well, there were about ten nuns at the school who offered to accompany us and help us. I took this course for a month and developed a really good friendship with these nuns.

It was the first time I had ever seen nuns. Before my Baptism, I was closed off in my own little world, with my family, my things, and school. But becoming a committed young Catholic opened me up to others; my group of friends grew much larger; I met many people and discovered many new things. Faith broadens your horizons and opens you up to relationships with others, not just with God. This was true for the nuns as well: They had seemed distant before, but now I knew them closely. They grew very fond of me and would sometimes say, "Lazarus, perhaps you could go to the seminary." I would obviously say no, but those words were the first I heard about the seminary, and they kept coming back to my mind. Religious women have been very important in my faith journey. And, speaking of role models, I began to be fascinated by Andrew Kim. He was only twenty-five years old [when martyred], and I was saying to myself, "It's worth living life like this." His testimony made me see how concrete Christianity is. It helps you to live life in this beautiful, big, bright way. It helps you not to waste it. And so, I felt the desire to attend

Holy Mass every day. To do so before school, I would go at six in the morning. I would leave early, in the cold, in the rain—always. The nuns, of course, were very happy!

The Desire for the Priesthood

Gradually the desire to follow the path of the priesthood grew within me. In Korea, one can enter the major seminary three years after receiving Baptism, but I had been baptized more recently. Even in this circumstance, however, I could see God's providence. My pastor, encouraged by the sisters, had told the seminary vice-rector of the seriousness of my commitment and how, even as a young boy, I used to attend Mass every day early in the morning. And so, I went for the interview. Meanwhile, it had happened that half of the expected seminarians did not appear. In Korea, to enter the University—or to move from minor to major seminary—you have to take an exam, and some future seminarians had failed it. So, enrollments were low in the seminary, and the vice-rector, encouraged by the references for me, took me in anyway. This experience was of great help to me later on. The Lord used it to teach me that rules are important, but that people's lives are more important than rules, and that we must be able to look deeper and with a broader perspective. According to the rules, I should not have been allowed to enter the seminary, but the discernment of the sisters, the parish priest, and the vice-rector went beyond the rules. When, many years later, I became seminary rector, I remembered this life lesson many times while discerning and evaluating the vocational journey of seminarians. Grace has the first place in spiritual life and discernment, before our rules.

My decision [to enter the seminary] was not well received by my family. At first, I said nothing and took the university entrance exam as if I were applying to any other faculty. Of course, my choice later came to light. No one was happy. My mother cried for three days, without eating or sleeping. I am the youngest child; she dreamed of me going to university. She had put money aside for me. Most importantly, for many people, celibacy was inconceivable. Today, many people do not marry, but back then, in Korea, it was unusual for someone to remain celibate. Yet, in a short time, the Lord transformed her inner feelings. She first went to her cousin, who had been my high school teacher, and he told her about my serenity on the road to the priesthood. Then—more importantly—she approached the Catholic Church and was very impressed by the beauty and the joy of the people who attended. Two months later, she also received Baptism. And then, she became an apostle of evangelization. As Pope Francis often said, faith is also transmitted by contagion, by the joy we know how to convey. This is a bit of the story of my childhood, my family, discovering faith, and then the priesthood.

Today, the family context in Asia, including Korea, is changing. Once I went to my friend's house for Sunday lunch. We sat down at the table, and he, together with his wife and his many children, began to pray before eating. Seeing that simple gesture lived by everyone with normality and participation, I said to myself, Someday

I want to have a family like this! This was normal in Korean Catholic families, where the faith was passed on with joy and as an important part of human growth and life. Today, all this risks being lost in an unhelpful culture that has brought into the people's hearts another vision: materialism and competition. If Christianity invites us to become like Jesus, to be welcoming as he is, and to inaugurate in his love a fraternal coexistence, exaggerated competition instead closes us in on ourselves, and others become obstacles to be overcome, because everyone wants to be first. The other is no longer my brother or sister.

There remains a widespread common sense, almost a religious sense in Asian, including Korean, people. They are particularly interested when it comes to promoting charity toward others, as was done during the Covid 19 pandemic and with the vaccinations, including some specific proposals that I put forward in the Bishops' Conference. In these cases, people look kindly on the Church and participate generously and joyfully. Even many nonbelievers get involved. Charity is very attractive. In a society that is materialistic and competitive, thus individualistic, whenever people are challenged by Christian charity to broaden their relationships and leave their comfort zones, they are attracted to the Church. Thus, we need a Church that testifies to the importance of fraternity and mutual love, as well as to paying attention to those in need. At the same time, the Church is well aware that the problems of the crisis of faith in today's families have deep roots. It is children and young people who must be accompanied during their growth in the discovery of faith, so that they do not reach adulthood and marriage as people indifferent to God. A film about Saint Andrew Kim is almost ready, and when I saw a preview, one thing was on my mind: "I have a dream, not only for the young people of Korea, but for those of the whole world, that they may live their lives like this." For this to happen, we don't need to do great things; rather we need to carry on with the little things of everyday life. This has also been my story: God makes use of all that we are and all that we make available to him.

The Encounter with Jesus

An Unexpected Joy that Accompanies Everyday Life

In the humble and sometimes monotonous valley of the everyday, where our daily lives flow silently or tumultuously with their activities, struggles, and hopes, an encounter with Jesus can open new horizons and ignite a new way of imagining our existence and the reality that surrounds us. On the other hand, this was the greatest "revolution" of Jesus, underpinned, above all, by the beauty of his parables: to free each of us from the prison of our own ego, to broaden the horizons of our imagination, and to enable us to embrace life in a new way.

⌒

*When and how did this happen in your life?
Why was the discovery of Jesus fascinating?*

My story is so simple, so ordinary, that even the encounter with Jesus and my friendship with him are not tied to any specific or extraordinary event. It took place in ordinary situations and, especially, through the people who somehow opened my heart to this knowledge. I am more grateful to the concrete witnesses I met along the way than to any particular event. Of these witnesses, we can say, one was physically distant but incredibly close to my dreams and ideals: He was Andrew Kim, who was then blessed; he was a young man, a strong, courageous, heroic guy with an adventurous life that he lived to the fullest. And that attracted me: I dreamed of becoming like him. Other witnesses, on the other hand, were physically close and helped me take hold of my dream, to make it concrete in my life choices; among these were especially the nuns, who loved me, introduced me to Jesus, and proclaimed the faith and, sometimes, invited me to reflect on the choice of the priestly life. This is a valuable lesson for the spiritual life: It often begins with attraction because we are fascinated by the life, freedom, and courage of some saint or person we know and who is close to us; and so we begin to dream, to have great ideals, perhaps to desire to offer our whole life to the Lord and to devote ourselves totally to others, as the Gospel asks us. But after this first phase of idealism, which is beautiful but perhaps a bit too lofty, we realize that real life is fought not so much at the heights of our ideals as on the plains of everyday life. And there our dreams and ideals must take shape in the situations and choices of each day.

If we do not want our ideals of the spiritual life to remain abstract and never realized, it is necessary, at some point, to "come down from the clouds" and seek the way to make them concrete and alive in real life. And for this, we need to be accompanied by someone who takes us by the hand. For me, it was, above all, the nuns.

The Crisis: A Place of Encounter with God

Then, in the concrete situations of my life, I discovered a hidden but surprising presence of the Lord. First of all, he presented himself immediately during a moment of crisis. When I entered the seminary, I dreamed of paradise; I thought everything there was beautiful. I knew nothing about that life. I had only recently discovered Christianity, so when I entered and saw several boys dressed in priests' shirts, I asked why there were all those priests. And a friend of mine looked at me in amazement, wondering how someone who knew nothing about the seminary life could decide to come here and embark on this journey. So, you see, I thought everything was perfect—a problem-free environment, where you could breathe holiness. This was perhaps a little too grand an ideal compared to reality, but it only took a few days to realize that I had been wrong and to understand that it was a place like any other, with all the contradictions that we human beings carry within us. It was a moment of crisis, and I asked the Lord what I should do. Certainly, I could not return home after leaving my family behind with many hardships to follow this path.

A few days later, a conference took place in the seminary that was offered as a time of formation. A Focolare priest and two lay people, also Focolare members, came to speak to us, sharing how they lived Christianity, how they lived the Word of God. It was a shock for me because until then I had been content to contemplate the beauty of the Gospel and of the Word from a distance without integrating it into my everyday life, and therefore it had no tangible effect. One of them shared that he worked at a school and lived in the adjoining boarding house, where his landlady was a woman who had a very stern demeanor at all times—let's say a somewhat harsh woman. Living the Word of God meant showing love to that woman too. However, love is made up of concrete signs, too, otherwise, it remains only a good idea. So he simply started to greet and to smile at her. That woman was never greeted by anyone; she was only feared. Slowly, her attitude changed. At that moment, I felt that the Gospel is very close to life, within the little things that we encounter every day and are called to welcome or face. They concluded the conference by inviting those who wanted to participate in a meeting the following Sunday. It took place in Seoul, and I chose to go. I had a good time that day, and on my way back to the seminary, I found out that some seminarians were meeting each week around the Word of Life. And I began to attend that group as well.

Living the Word

The Word was not only meditated upon or prayed, but echoed, in the small things of community life, even in the small services that we undertook to put into practice Jesus' commandment. Well, I began to feel that the seminary was very good; suddenly, my former negative view disappeared. I understood that very often the judgments we make about reality, even ecclesial reality, and the unease we experience, with all the anxieties and agitation, are not always real and justified; they often depend on the inner "lenses" we use, on our points of view, on how we look at things. The seminary had ceased to be an unpleasant place simply because it did not correspond to my ideal of perfection; now it was a community, with its lights and shadows, but I felt at home there and at peace because my attitude had changed. I lived there and experienced [the seminary life] starting from the Word of God and, therefore, in a daily commitment to love and joyful service. For me, this was a true encounter with Jesus.

This experience of "living the Word" stayed with me even afterward, for example, during my military service. In Korea, even those who choose the priesthood are called to military service. I served for thirty-two months and was sent to a dangerous zone, near the border with North Korea. There was, obviously, no celebration of Sunday Mass. I began to ask myself questions about my identity as a Christian and about attending the Sunday Mass. I had to find a way, but in the end, I began to think, What does it really mean to be a Christian? When am I a Christian? First and foremost, when I live the Gospel of the Lord. And so, with much courage, I went to the higher military authority to ask permission for some of us to gather on Sunday to have a meeting around the Word of God.

We were granted permission and started with four people, in a corner of the dining hall. We could not celebrate Mass, but we celebrated the Liturgy of the Word. Those four became five, then ten. And finally, at Christmas that year, twenty people received Baptism. It was for me another great sign of the presence of Jesus in my life. He had not appeared in special or religious circumstances but while I was living an experience like the military service, in a place that was not very peaceful, with few comforts, with not even the ability to celebrate Sunday Mass. Yet, once again, he had come to me in the Word, and that weekly liturgy had brought others closer to the faith; it had been an instrument of evangelization.

Perhaps today we also need to ask ourselves some questions about the liturgies we celebrate and whether the number of Masses we schedule corresponds to an opportunity to get to know the Lord truly and closely; whether they are a privileged way to discover the faith or a habit, whether they convey the living Word of the Lord that touches lives or are reduced to a repetition just to satisfy a precept. Christianity is not to fulfill a cultic and moral obligation; it is first and foremost about allowing oneself to be reached, questioned, and touched by the Word of the Lord.

Even in this experience, concrete actions to "live the Word" were vital. We were marching through the night and for many kilometers, with our backpacks on our shoulders. I saw that one of my companions was very tired, and so I offered to carry his rifle, which was quite heavy. A little later, during a break, that friend asked me why everyone else was tired and dejected, yet I, on the other hand, was happy. Of course, I was tired too, but perhaps my faith and the encounter with Jesus offered me the strength to be inwardly serene, which was visible on the outside. I spoke to that person about Jesus, and he also received Baptism. When others see our joy as Christians, they are inspired by it.

The Frascati Experience

By the time I finished my military service, the Focolare had opened a center in Seoul, which I frequented. Then I received an invitation from Rome to continue my journey in Frascati [near

Rome], in the house of formation for Focolarini. My bishop granted me permission, and thus I had a third significant experience of my real encounter with Jesus. I left Korea with a few dollars in my pocket, but I had been told that there, in Frascati, they lived by putting everything in common. When I arrived [at the airport] in Fiumicino, I felt a little lost in a country I didn't know. I was looking for someone to pick me up, but I couldn't find anyone. I approached a young man to ask for information, and he was immediately very kind. When he understood where I needed to go, to my surprise, he told me that he was a seminarian returning from the Holy Land. He knew well the priests who had invited me to the Frascati house, and he accompanied me there. I arrived without a problem and without spending a single dollar! Once again, the Lord did not reveal himself in a spectacular way but by allowing me to experience love of neighbor, generous help, and a warm welcome along my journey.

In Frascati, together with about ninety people, between priests and seminarians, the experience I lived led me to an important conclusion about faith. The only book is Sacred Scripture. The only law is the new commandment. The only Master is Jesus. When we place this at the foundation of our journey of faith, the rest comes as a result, as a gift and a grace.

Therefore, living the Word in everyday situations and living gratuitous love in mutual sharing are, for me, two privileged ways to encounter Jesus and to know the Gospel. Christianity is not a matter of ideas. It is an experience that communicates joy to us through making us feel loved by God and by our brothers and sisters. And so it sustains our journey. When people who are approaching the faith or those who are experiencing some spiritual difficulty ask me a question, I just say, begin by putting the Word into your life—in the small things, small everyday gestures, small commitments. And that Word then enlightens and shows the way, because if you live the Word in your life, you realize that Jesus is in your brothers [and sisters], and you also develop the desire to encounter him in the Sacraments. This is central for me even today. When I do my examination of conscience in the evening, I ask myself what my relationship with Jesus has been that day, present in the Word, in the Sacraments, and in my brothers and sisters.

This is why I immediately felt in tune with Pope Francis, because from the very beginning he has called us back to the Gospel: Turn toward the Gospel; rediscover the Gospel! And his way of preaching was a way that led to the discovery of the Gospel. When he proclaimed the Word, Pope Francis always showed that if we put the love that Jesus teaches us in the little things, they become big things. And this stirs admiration. Living the Gospel is this: living love in all the little things because love calls for love; that is, it breaks down our loneliness, generates good relationships, and transforms the life and the society in which we live.

For me, this centrality of the Word is necessary in the Church. What I have seen in recent years in Korea, for example, among candidates for the priesthood, is that young men who already had contact with the Word presented themselves with a "foundation" that was prepared and predisposed compared to others. There needs to be more space for the Word in the diverse expressions of Christianity. It seems to me that we sometimes approach issues in the life of the Church and situations of people with a predominantly legal or moral emphasis, while a more pastoral and spiritual approach based on an evangelical attitude is lacking. Doctrine, law, and morality are a consequence of the Gospel; they do not come first.

Love: A Fundamental Criterion

If we accept this view, we realize that the most important thing, when we are faced with the world's challenges or with people's most difficult existential situations, is dialogue. If we take the Gospel as our starting point and goal, then, after entering into dialogue, we interpret everything from the heart of the commandment of love, which is the heart of everything. This is the fundamental criterion: love. When I was still in Korea, a Vatican journalist once asked me what I thought about divorced couples who remarried. I felt compelled to say, looking at the Gospel, the only absolute value for me is love, which remains even in heaven. Everything must be interpreted from this point of view, even if other things are somewhat sacrificed. All situations must be viewed in relation to this criterion and not to a moral norm or a canonical law. One can go through life perhaps not having "everything in order" from the point of view of the Christian law, but still having the desire to walk, to question oneself, to change, and, at the same time, live in a situation where there is room for love. There, then, is an acceptance of the Gospel, and a flame of divine grace that we must not extinguish with rigid judgment. And the secret of love is the Cross. While Jesus stretched out his arms, our life situation was not in accordance with the perfection of law or morality. Quite the contrary. At that moment, before Jesus, we were lost, and with his cry—"My God, my God, why have you forsaken me?"—he says that in some way, he too has "lost" God. In that narrow passage, in that extreme situation, Jesus gives us all the love possible; he gives himself with love to snatch us from death. Why should the Church do otherwise?

Love first, then everything else: This is what I try to live, from the moment I met Jesus.

The encounter with Jesus, and the Gospel at the center of our lives—let me make one last point—fills us with an unexpected joy that sustains us on our journey, and that we are also able to communicate to others. I spent six months in Boston learning English. Americans, somewhat out of habit, ate a lot of food, or rather, they put a lot of different foods on their plates and then left half of them uneaten. For me, this was scandalous. I would leave my plate empty and take something from what they left behind—until someone asked me why. I said, many people are dying of hunger in the world, and this is a grave sin! From that moment on, some of them began to take a little less to consider how much was necessary and what was superfluous. This experience is better than many sermons. The Gospel of love, of attention to the poor, and of sharing, had been proclaimed, and immediately it became life in a precise and concrete sign: Taking less to throw away less food!

In the end, there in Boston, they gave me a kind of title: "You make me happy!" This is a call for Christians: Living the Gospel means making others happy, bringing them in contact with God's infinite love, which fills the steps of our journey with hope.

A "Dialogue" Between Heaven and Earth

Training Priests in Relationships

In many ways, encountering Jesus can trans-form our lives. The beauty of the Christian God, whose face Jesus showed us, also lies in his discreet coming toward us, in that kind-ness that always gently gathers what we are and what we have, without forcing anyone or compelling anyone to do anything. He is not a God who puts us in a straitjacket and demands military obedience, but a Father of love who supports and accompanies us, without humiliating us in any way, welcom-ing us for the little that we are, inviting us to broaden the horizons of our hearts so that we grow and open ourselves to the mystery of joy. This is why, as we see in the Gospels, Jesus' calls to conversion are not meant to devalue who we are but to transform our potential and open it to the service of God and our brothers and sisters, so that it may grow and multiply. Jesus does not tell Peter to do something else but to go beyond simply fishing for a living, and to become a fisher of men. Among the many calls, the many ways of being a disciple of the Lord, there is consecration to the priestly ministry. Even the story of a cardinal begins from there, on that day when the Lord's eyes rested on him and—as Pope Francis has often shared when speaking of his vocation—that merciful gaze became the center of attraction for his whole life.

Let's talk about your journey to the priesthood, Fr. Lazarus, your memories of the seminary, and what you consider important and essential now that you are Prefect of the Dicastery for the Clergy.

For me, the seminary was a big family where one could learn to love and follow Jesus in a concrete way and as a choice of life, or at least, that was what I thought. However, I must say that, in Korea, the seminary was a place where you felt very strongly the weight of hierarchical authority because, as it happens everywhere, it was a reflection of Korean society and its culture, which is particularly based on the authority of those who are older and those who hold positions of leadership. We have inherited this aspect, as a basic vision, from Confucianism: In that reality, age counts for a lot because those who are older are more mature, just as position and role matter a lot. Hierarchy is very important: Sometimes, greater age automatically implies that a person must be obeyed. The late Cardinal Stephen Kim, whose beatification process is about to begin, is said to have remarked with a touch of irony after his retirement: I am Catholic, but I see my life influenced more by the teachings of Confucius than by anyone else!

This atmosphere was also very noticeable in the seminary, and it had a particularly strong effect on me because, as I have already said, I had not grown up in the

Catholic Church. I certainly lived in Korean society; I had experienced strict obedience in military life, but I was not prepared, for example, to obey a priest. What helped me mature in all this was the heart of the Gospel, the commandment of love, because gradually I became convinced that love conquers all and overcomes everything, even ranks, roles, and hierarchies. When Jesus sent out the apostles, he sent them two by two, so that they could experience the new commandment and proclaim the Gospel, first and foremost through the witness of brotherhood and charity. For us, even in Christian and priestly formation, as in seminaries, the model must be the first community that was formed after Jesus: They lived around the Word, sharing everything. The main authority was that of the Word. In general, in the Church, we should remember this: It is better to be imperfect but in communion than to be perfect in disunity. Therefore, hierarchical roles should never create a distance that divides or serve as badges of perfection to those who hold them. If the life of the people and the commandment of love do not come before roles, we fall into ideology. In Korea, Christianity has also made a significant contribution in this regard. Contrary to what is often said, especially in the West, a certain macho, patriarchal, and strongly hierarchical culture has been challenged by Christianity, and Christians have contributed a lot to the growth of the idea of equality and dignity for all people. Some time ago, there was a strong separation between different social classes; people could not even eat together if they were not of the same class. But when someone converted to Christianity and received Baptism, they immediately discovered the beauty of being together and sharing a meal, not only the Eucharistic one, without distinction of class. This gradually introduced into that culture a new seed, a fraternal vision, helping to improve relations between different generations, which were quite complex. This is a concrete transformation that the Gospel brings to real life and also to society. Culture may well affirm the right of the greatest, the most adult, and the strongest, but Jesus praises the little ones, the children who had no rights at that time, and elevates them as models for all of us. Thus, we all learn from Jesus that we must see each other as brothers and sisters. Before anything else, brothers and sisters.

Freedom at the Center of Church Relationships

My experience in the seminary in Frascati, in Italy, made me see yet another reality regarding hierarchical relationships within the Church. For me, it was an important experience, which the Lord asked me to treasure by calling me, many years later, to become rector of the seminary. Although it was not easy because it involved challenging a characteristic element of our culture and society, as rector, I slowly tried to create a climate of relational trust. Every seminarian could feel free—serene even—when expressing some fragility or some mistakes made along the way, through frank and authentic educational dialogue. After several years, I heard from some that they had a joyful experience in the seminary, and that they had found it to be a better and freer environment than what was the case on the outside. I am really very happy about this.

I believe that this is important and necessary in all ecclesial relationships. We are called to help people be free, grow in freedom, reflect on their mistakes and desire to change, not by constraining them or stifling them, but precisely by offering them a space in which they can be themselves, knowing that they are loved and not judged. Especially in seminaries, if there is one thing we have to be careful about, it is the way we establish the relationship between educators and seminarians and offer the "rule of life" of the community. We can set up a relational model based on fear, performance, and observance of rules; then, obedience becomes external, based only on external aspects and, at worst, on the desire to please superiors. But in this way, we create very problematic personalities who tomorrow will continue to play the role of formal obedience with the bishop and will end up doing so even in their relationship with the Lord and with the demands of priestly life. There is a risk, that is, of superficial belonging, without internalization, without real motivation, without authenticity.

I, for example, had a bishop who, in the exercise of authority, was very strict. If one asked for an appointment with him, the first thing he asked was, What is the problem? Several times, I answered that there was no problem but only a desire to say hello, to talk. This was also helpful to me because, later as a bishop, I never asked a priest I was receiving, What is the problem? but always started by offering coffee or lunch, because no authority is possible without first opening up spaces of sincere and cordial dialogue.

Seminary Life, and "Death" on Ordination Day

As might be evident, I have always been helped by my character, my willingness to compromise and engage in dialogue, even in the most difficult situations. Consequently, as a seminarian, I benefited from my time at the seminary. At that time, even though the image of the good shepherd was used as always, in reality, there was a precise image of the priest: He was seen as a teacher of truth and doctrine, and therefore, one was formed according to this image. However, over time, also thanks to the development of the Magisterium—I am thinking, for example, of *Pastores dabo vobis*—things have slowly changed. As rector, I have tried to present the image of the priest as a man of communion, anchored to the one priest who is Jesus, whose priesthood is consummated, above all, on the Cross, on that altar where he brings about peace between us and God. And being a promoter of communion does not exclude teaching the truth. Rather he proposes it and helps it to be realized from within relationships animated by love and by a journey that is made together, consisting of mutual listening and dialogue. On the Cross, Jesus establishes a dialogue between heaven and earth, and this also means dying, offering himself. Being a teacher can mean teaching from "without": without passion, without getting involved in the life of others, without having the other's faith and happiness at heart. The priest instead dies for others; he offers the priestly sacrifice by offering himself, giving first and foremost himself. A man of dialogue, of closeness, of communion, he is called to die like Jesus, to give his life for others.

In this regard, I cannot forget what happened to me on the day I was ordained. I woke up in the morning, and I do not know why, perhaps something related to my sleep, I had the feeling that on that day I would die. I wondered how it was possible that, on the day of my ordination, I could have this strange feeling and could even die. But perhaps that was an inner warning from the Spirit because when I prostrated myself during the Mass and the assembly invoked the saints, I suddenly understood, and I reinterpreted that feeling I had had in the morning. I was indeed prostrate; I was like the grain of wheat that falls to the ground and dies; I was in the position of dying with Christ for the sake of my brothers and sisters. In that moment, I understood: The priesthood means dying so as to live with Jesus for one's brothers and sisters. And I tried to put that into practice and to pass it on even as a rector. I myself was committed to being a man of dialogue. When I met monthly with the seminarians, a climate of freedom slowly developed; questions were asked; we interacted, seeking together to discern the way forward. All relationships in the Church grow only in this way, in communion.

Formation for the Priesthood: The Human and Emotional Maturity of Candidates

Very important for priestly formation is that seminarians can see communion in the Church, beginning with that between formators and between bishops. At the same time, it is important that seminarians experience a sense of closeness from the Church, especially from their pastors. How can they be close and compassionate if, apart from their studies and other knowledge, they have never experienced firsthand any attention given to them? As bishop, I used to go to the seminary every year and live with the seminarians for three days. Gradually, other bishops who did not do this, partly because of the distance, began to think about and promote moments of communion and closeness with their seminarians.

The same applies to the life of prayer. It is clear that prayer, not so much the recitation of prayers to fulfill a discipline, but an openness and relationship with the Lord, remains the foundation of priestly formation. But it is also obvious that seminarians learn the spirit of prayer, the attitude of a heart open to prayer, by seeing their formators pray and, above all, by having priests and formators who are people of prayer as their companions on the journey. In this area too, there is a high risk that the spiritual life is a kind of outward garb, that religious duties will be performed, but that priests will not become men in love with the Word, capable of silence, of setting aside time for dialogue with the Lord.

Of course, different aspects must be balanced in the life of a priest. Prayer is one of the pillars of formation because it is the foundation of spiritual life, but this does not detract from the importance of intellectual formation and study. In Korea, this was very important, but I believe it should be important for everyone today. We need well-educated priests, who are capable of thinking and are equipped with critical thinking skills to face the ever-new challenges that the world presents to us.

Then, I believe there is one more thing of fundamental importance. In addition to recommending prayer and study, there is strong emphasis on human and emotional maturity, and this is certainly important. If we do not have people who are balanced in terms of their relationship with themselves and with others, capable of experiencing emotions and feelings in a balanced way, we will always have serious problems in priestly life. However, I feel that today we must add another aspect: missionary maturity and community maturity. The new pastoral challenges and the different ecclesial and cultural situations we encounter require us to take a leap forward. We need priests who are "trained for mission"; that is, who acquire a missionary spirit with that inner flexibility and pastoral availability that enable them to get involved creatively in an exercise of ministry that, in some ways, could be innovative and adaptable, that in today's world could be more elastic and less static—a ministry truly oriented toward the genuine needs of evangelization and not simply the preservation of existing practice. At the same time, we also need to grow in the communitarian dimension of priestly life and ministry.

In seminary life, one is, in some ways, very protected because one lives within a relational context in which prayer is supported by a rule of daily and weekly life, which is marked by rhythmic times that are, in turn, drawn from days that are, all things considered, well organized. Then, it happens more and more often that when we become immersed in pastoral life, and even before that, in the simple management of daily life, in everyday tasks, in the continuous overexposure to which our souls are forced even by the simple use of technology and social communication, then the time and space—but I would like to say, the inner disposition itself—for prayer is reduced. Gradually, Eucharistic adoration, meditation on the Word, and then even the breviary are abandoned. This is not out of ill will; sometimes the rhythms of prayer no longer fit with the form that priestly life and apostolic ministry have taken today, compared to a society that was organized differently, in a somewhat less complex pastoral and ecclesial manner. We can say this: In the seminary, the dimension of spiritual life follows a rule, but the ultimate goal is to prepare for the future or, better said, to root the person in this reality so that it becomes natural when he becomes a priest. Today, this relationship between the seminary and the future is increasingly difficult and cannot be taken for granted. I believe we should look more closely and tenderly at what flows in the heart of a priest: loneliness, anxiety about performance, inner struggles, along with common human frailties. And in all this, constancy in prayer and spiritual life is not easy. This is why I say that today, a seminarian should also be "tested" on his communal maturity because, as priests, we will increasingly need to work in communion, in many cases to think and carry out pastoral ministry together, to live in community even though we are diocesan priests, and thus, receive human and spiritual support, that is, the support of friendship, comparing of notes, dialogue, and sharing in the apostolic mission. The common work of priests should not be thought of only when there are vocational problems or pastoral needs, but as a distinctive trait of the priest.

And this is a Gospel witness we can give today. Jesus sends them out two by two, and the disciple's credibility comes first and foremost from the love he lives with his brothers, before words or teachings. And so, the image of the man of relationship returns—with God but also with his brothers.

The Priest and Relationships

All this, of course, must be accompanied by a serene ability to relate to others that, beginning with our time in the seminary, helps us to overcome the idea of the priest as "separate": We are called to live relationships—not only pastoral but also friendly—with people, with families, with youth, and simply, like everyone else, but living those relationships with a quality that, obviously, is proper to our faith and our state of life. This must become an important element of discernment in priestly formation. If a seminarian has difficulties in his human relationships, it is necessary to intervene and to do everything to help him mature, reflecting carefully before allowing him to proceed to ordination. To this end, I believe we need to take a more decisive step on the presence of women in seminaries—not just in words, not just as an accessory, but as an integral part of the formation process. In Korea, when I was rector of the seminary, from 1998 to 2003, there was a nun among the formators. Her presence greatly helped the emotional formation and relational maturation of the seminarians.

Of course, this requires us to continually reform the seminaries. I believe that they still can be places of formation, especially because of the community aspect that they are able to guarantee much more than other "places of faith." This also means that we cannot keep educational institutions running with very few people because this does not guarantee a high quality of formation. At the same time, however, the seminary should not be a "separate" place and time, but rather a space where we learn to network, to connect, and to mature in relationship. All this is not possible unless we overcome another obstacle to communion—that between bishops, and also that between formators. Division, the defense of one's own little world, the difficulty of seeking a common goal and common tools to achieve it, greatly damages priestly formation.

These are the two important aspects: to be men of communion, and thus men of mission toward others. Ultimately, this is also a specific trait of Jesus—a man of communion with the Father and, therefore, driven by love for his brothers and sisters.

Beyond Clericalism

Being a Priest Today

*T*alking about the priesthood is an arduous undertaking, at least for two kinds of reasons, one arguably more objective and the other more historical-temporal. The first shows the distance, which can never be bridged, between all that the priest is called to live and represent, and his fragile humanity in which the gift of vocation is grafted. The disproportion between the grace received and the actual correspondence of real priestly life remains. The second, more historical-temporal reason, concerns our present day. Talking about the priesthood today, amidst outdated models, nostalgia for the past, uncertainty of identity, generalized and widespread crises that affect the priest and reflect the broader ecclesial crisis underway, is difficult and at times depressing. To untangle the knot, the fundamental question concerning the identity of the priest should always return to ecclesial reflections: What did Jesus really want when he gathered around him the Apostles and sent them on mission? Is the priest an evangelizer or a bureaucrat? A pastor or a functionary? On such questions, Pope Francis' prophetic word is more illuminating than any other analysis. Certainly, being a priest has to do with the model of Church that, in so many ways, we generate. An autocratic Church that stands high above the world inevitably corresponds to a priest who resembles more a military leader than a shepherd, more a lord of the Roman Empire than an apostle of the Gospel. Certainly, against this and other temptations, it is necessary to allow oneself to be challenged and changed by the provocation of the Gospel.

᠆

You became a priest in the late 1970s, Fr. Lazarus. Society—the Korean and Asian society—had a strong sense of authority, and priests were considered superior and detached from the rest of the people, despite the instructions of the Second Vatican Council. Can you tell us about the beginning of your priestly journey? How did you experience the priesthood? What do you think of being a priest? What are the challenges and difficulties today?

I became a priest in 1979. As already mentioned, my first strong experience was right that morning, when I had the feeling of dying, and I could not explain why. When I prostrated myself during the liturgy for the Ordination, I understood that to be a priest means to die with Christ, to offer one's life for him, with him, and like him. At that moment, I felt the presence of Jesus next to me, and I understood this fascinating mystery of priestly life. It is when we are prostrate, when we are "on the floor," when we are exposed and vulnerable and in contact with our true humanity and with our radical poverty; at that very moment, we can feel strongly the closeness and presence of the Lord in our lives and next to us because we are stripped of everything: of all claims, of all merit, of all idolatry, of self; and, in poverty, we open ourselves to encounter Jesus. Saint Paul reminds us of this with his rich theology on the mystery of Christ and the life of the Christian: "When I am weak, that is when I am strong" (2 Cor 12:10). When I returned to the sacristy after the ordination Mass, a priest gave me a small cross that I still wear and have never taken off, for in handing it to me he said, "Lazarus, this is your spouse for life." But this is not a spiritual idea or fad. To be a spouse is to die for the beloved, to make space, to be poor in order to be enriched by the other. And this is the spousal mystery inherent in the life of the beloved, in the relationship of the Christian with his Lord, and, in a different form, that of the priest with Jesus. At the same time, this dimension should not lead us to a form of disembodied mysticism; to be a spouse means to be a part of and father of a family. When we become priests, we bind ourselves to Jesus, but so as to bind ourselves to our brothers, to the family of the Church. I was able to experience all this in Frascati, where I studied, with many friends from Korea, and also with people of other faiths or religions. And one last thing, to clarify the concreteness of being a spouse: It means that the ultimate goal of our life is not the priesthood, but it is the Lord. He who loves and marries a person no longer thinks of himself; his ultimate goal is not even marriage but the encounter with the beloved, his love, his happiness. This is how it should be for us as well. The ultimate goal of our life is not to become a priest or being a priest in one way or another, but the courage and joy of choosing Jesus, the bridegroom, every day. And then again, every day, always, with enthusiasm. Whatever the path, whatever ministry we do, whatever set of personal and pastoral situations we experience, the most important thing for a priest is to ask himself every day: What am I choosing? Because even with the best of intentions, a priest can choose so many things and forget to make, to repeat, to renew the choice of God every day.

Overcoming the Plague of Clericalism

The above perspective, at least in terms of a personal and spiritual life, would also help overcome the scourge of clericalism that Pope Francis often denounced. If the goal is, indeed, the encounter with Jesus and, thus, to receive his love that makes us holy, we realize that the main vocation of our life is not ordained priesthood, but holiness. This is the call that is addressed to us in Baptism. Being a priest is the form and manner in which we are called to live [our] Baptism. From this profound conviction, if we allow it to be imprinted in our spiritual life, also at the pastoral and institutional level, a true reform of the ordained ministry could derive, no longer focused on the role, no longer imagined as "separate" from others, but experienced as a way of concretely living the Gospel, in service to God and to our brothers and sisters. The tendency, so widespread today, to revert to the past, to feel regret for a world that has now disappeared, and to look backward, perhaps even by displaying a series of external symbols and particular clothing, is in reality a symptom of a difficulty: We struggle to think of ourselves together and with others, while it gives us security and strengthens our identity to think of ourselves as separate, superior, almost chosen by God in a special way. Behind the nostalgia for traditionalism is the desire to return to a society in which the priest was "somebody." But this means that I need the external role to appreciate myself, to consider myself worthy of something. It is an anthropological fragility to watch out for from the very beginning, from the moment the signs of vocation appear. And I would add: Sometimes we think that small, so to speak "external" signs do little harm, or someone places them to mark the difference from others. But, in reality, it always starts with the small signs. Why drive around in fancy cars with drivers and other signs of power to show off to others? We keep justifying ourselves by saying that "these things have no impact" on living a simple lifestyle, being poor, being essential, walking with everyone else. I think, instead, that while, certainly, attention to these things alone does not solve our problems, we still start with these concrete things.

I remember—just to share something funny—once I went to the university in Korea for an event and, being rector of the seminary, I had a reserved parking space. But because I showed up without a driver and in a plain car, they wouldn't let me through to park. They didn't believe that I, too, was among the authorities! In fact, they thought I was someone's driver! It means that in the imagination, even that of the Church, authority is always accompanied by visible signs of power and wealth. This is not good. And in this, we must have the courage to go against the current. Not by doing extraordinary things, but simply by being like others, like ordinary people. Yet, to make choices like that takes spiritual strength.

The Spiritual Life of the Priest

On the other hand, the main foundation of priestly life is the spiritual life, without which it is not easy to live the ministry and face the daily challenges. When I became a priest, I remember that in the diocese there was a conflict between the priests and the bishop;

the latter, even though I had been requested as a professor in Seoul, did not want to let me go, asking me to be included in the diocesan pastoral work and, for a number of reasons, the cathedral being vacant, he sent me there as deputy pastor. A young man, newly ordained, sent to the cathedral: You can imagine what this sparked, especially among the older priests. These are challenges in the life of a priest, which can present themselves from the earliest moments. One enters into a diocese perhaps wounded by some problems, into a divided presbyterate, into a cultural situation and vision of the Church that does not always make room for the talent of young people, and so on. Without the underlying serenity and confidence that come from the spiritual life and from having anchored one's certainties in God, it is not easy to resist the gusts of these winds. We should not idealize the priesthood with abstract talk. A priest becomes a priest in a precise moment in the life of the Church. He immerses himself in a particular Church. He lives in one historical time and not in another. And he must know that, in all this, there is no lack of problems and difficulties because we are inside a history marked by fragility and still on the way to the whole truth.

I will add an important piece: The spiritual life, the attitude of trust in the Lord that a priest cultivates, generates an attitude that is essential for ministry—patience. We must be open to engage in everything, but then we must learn to wait for God's times that are better than ours. We have to trust how he leads history and leads it toward the good through that small faithfulness that we live out every day and that often seems to us to be useless. I say this with that very diocesan situation in mind. My bishop, in fact, shortly afterward became ill. One Sunday morning, after Mass, I went to visit him in the hospital, and he asked me what I had preached on. That day, the liturgy commemorated Saint Jerome and, in my homily, I had recalled the encounter in which the Lord had said to him, "Give me your sins." I found the courage to tell the bishop that perhaps he, too, had to set himself free, hand over his sins, give everything to Jesus. His eyes lit up, and he asked me to return the next day because he wanted me to hear his confession. He made a beautiful confession, and from that moment on, with a simple thank you, a phone call, a smile, a kind word, he began to mend the relationship with those priests with whom there had been hostility. Before he died, he even summoned the priest who was, in a way, leading the hostile group of priests. I stayed outside, and they talked for an hour, and the bishop died at the very end of that conversation. A real miracle, I would say, but with God's timing and through a little mediation that I managed to do. A priest must first and foremost work for reconciliation, to restitch together what has come apart. This is at the heart of the priestly ministry: to be a worker of mercy and reconciliation in the community, between different sensitivities, between people belonging to the same family, in the presbytery, and so on. And then to wait for God's timing, to let him carry out our plans for peace.

Taking Time for Yourself

There is something else that I have experienced in the priestly ministry that, unfortunately, is not very common among priests and is difficult to develop and accept. It may sound strange, but it is the ability—dare I say discipline—to take time for oneself, a time of rest and detachment from activities. I always took Monday as a personal day, after the labors of Sunday, and it was a time to rest, to meet other priests, to pray, and also to go to confession. There is a subtle risk in priestly life, that of diving headlong into activities and slowly convincing ourselves—in good faith, and even with spiritual motivation—that we are needed; that with all these commitments, we cannot afford to stray; that needs and work come first. Of course, we are called to offer our whole selves, our whole lives, and our time, with total availability; but this does not mean feeling that we are at the center of the mission and ministry or, even worse, feeling a scruple, a veiled sense of guilt, if we occasionally take some space for rest, to meet with friends or for recreation. This is even more true when it is a time to be with ourselves and lift our spirits in prayer. On this issue, I think we still have a somewhat rigid formation and, moreover, we run the risk of following the criteria of today's world: efficiency, performance, being active to always produce results, without ever slowing down our march. Many priests exhaust their physical, inner, and spiritual energies in precisely this way. The priest is not the center of the parish and the community; and indeed, many frustrations, sufferings, and depressions stem from the high demands we place on ourselves and our ministry. It takes inner freedom even to rest. But, of course, it takes courage to think and organize pastoral and ecclesial life ministry and collaboration with the lay faithful. Every priest must learn to take care of himself, his body, and his humanity. I remember truly, with much joy and emotion, that Chrism Mass during which Pope Francis, instead of giving the priests some other "duty" of spiritual or pastoral life to fulfill, wanted to recall with affectionate words "the weariness of priests" and to pray for them. And, among many valuable pointers, the Pope asks us an important question: "Can I rest from myself, from my self-demanding nature, from my self-satisfaction, from my self-referentiality?"

Priests, But Only Together

Along with the spiritual life and self-care, an important element in the life of the priest is the ability to collaborate, to work together. I was able to live this experience, first in the parish and then as rector of the seminary, and I can say that shared ministry is invaluable. It does not just lighten the load, which would be too weak a motivation. Instead, it grounds us in an evangelical lifestyle, sharpens our view of reality, in that we can see it with so many different eyes and, by comparing notes and practicing dialogue, it opens us to communion and also to the sweet consolation of friendship both with other priests and with the laity. It offers a witness of unity to the world. And it certainly offers greater possibilities for our pastoral action because we do not walk alone but share ideas, visions, and projects. In the current context, it is even more necessary to carry out pastoral work that is "networked," involving various actors in the area, so that it can be more effective and pervasive. This requires priests to be experts in humanity and capable of peaceful and constructive relationships with others.

So, I repeat: The most important thing in a priest's life is the choice of God, to be renewed every day. Without this, despite educational and pedagogical aids, we fail to develop this inner structure suitable for spiritual life, the care of one's life, and relationship with others, in the context of a not always easy priestly existence. The risk is that as long as we are somewhat stimulated by work, pastoral activity, or some demand or responsibility, we keep going. But when we stop, we begin to ask: Who am I? What should I do? We risk an inner emptiness, an identity crisis. The priest is not the "mover and shaker"; the priesthood is not an external profession separate from the person and his life. Only the one who is anchored in God and who chooses God every day can always start anew. He receives light, strength, courage, and the ability to face even failures, and to accept an occasional personal or pastoral defeat. And let's not think of this as something overly intimate. On the contrary, the fundamental relationship with God helps us to open ourselves to others and, therefore, to

experience those healthy and good friend-
ships and relationships that sustain priestly
life, the fatigue, the frustrations, and the joys
of ministry. Finding a good priest friend, a
family of friends, a few people with whom
we can be fully ourselves, even beyond the
role we play, is important, also, so as to inte-
grate the call to celibacy in a serene way and
without it throwing off balance other aspects
of our personality or habits. But all this is
possible precisely when we have an intimate
relationship with God, which slowly frees us
from selfishness, closures, and the risk of
thinking ourselves as self-sufficient by virtue
of the priesthood or pastoral assignment to
which we are called.

After all, this means abiding in him, in
his love. So—and I return for a moment to
the subject of weariness—we can face even
heavy and tiring days, and in the evening be
tired but feel our hearts at peace. To be tired
but happy. There is another tiredness that,
instead, consumes us, unnerves us, withers
us, and happens when we put ourselves at
the center and burden ourselves with many
demands, or elevate ourselves to the status

of heroes. The priest must not lose the center, which is Jesus. The rest—as the Gospel says—will be given to us in addition.

Being a Father, Being a Brother

Episcopal Ministry and Its Challenges

The life of the Christian community lives with the healthy tension between the importance of each person's active presence and the need for a ministry of synthesis and unity capable of harmonizing and guiding diverse voices and sensibilities.

Those who enter into the mystery of the Church know well that it is not a political expedient to try to survive and "run the show" but a fact of faith: Some the Lord chose as apostles, others as prophets, still others as teachers, and so on. The beauty of the Church, which often emerges even within the folds *of its many wrinkles, is precisely this: not uniformity or approval but—as Pope Francis has well reminded us—unity in diversity, the companionship of differences. Fascinating and uncomfortable, necessary and restless, then, is the ministry of the bishop: weaver of relationships, expert craftsman of unity, far-sighted prophet called to look far and encourage the sometimes weary steps of the people; he can never settle into the role or claim an authority separate from the fraternity. His main call is closeness to God and to the people.*

~

One day, the proposal for the episcopacy reached you, Fr. Lazarus. What can you tell us about the episcopal experience? What were the pivotal points of your ministry? What would you say to a bishop today, challenged by the expectations and hopes of the people, but also called to face challenges and problems?

When I was rector of the seminary in Korea, Msgr. Morandini was the Apostolic Nuncio. He wanted to meet me, and after we got to know each other, I began a relationship of trust with the Nunciature, especially concerning information that is necessary for a representative so as to know more about the local Church and its priests. I have always tried to respond freely and honestly for the good of the Church. But in this time of collaboration, often having to question my conscience about a bishop's qualities and virtues, without even realizing it, it is as if the Lord is preparing the way for me.

When I became a bishop, I immediately felt within myself that it was possible to live the ministry to which I had been called only by carrying the local Church on one shoulder and the universal Church on the other; that is, breathing with two lungs, because, even as bishops, we have to be attentive. There is not only one's own diocese, of which I may eventually feel like the head or, even worse, the owner. There is a portion of the Church that is part of a larger family and of the mystery of the universal Church, which implies the communion of a shepherd with other shepherds and with the Church of Rome. Without communion, there is no episcopate.

How the Lord Prepares the Way

Having been rector of the seminary also prepared me for episcopal ministry. During those years, I understood more and more that a process of spiritual and ecclesial formation and growth exists when true relationships are established and mutual closeness is experienced; that is, when the person comes before ideas and norms. Having developed such bonds in the seminary, as rector, helped me later. As a bishop, I always tried to be close to the lives of the priests, to congratulate them on their name day, to have a personal relationship with them, even if it was not so easy dealing with two hundred priests. For my part, I tried to always make room for the priests, over and above the established commitments. In fact, I have to confess that I had an official car of the diocese, but I also had a smaller car that I bought with my own money and drove only myself, to visit the priests from time to time confidentially.

No personal consideration is necessary because Pope Francis often recommends it—closeness. Above all, a bishop must live in closeness to priests, so that they are not considered as employees of a company that must function, but as sons and brothers in the faith and ministry. In the closeness to priests, sharing their pastoral successes or failures, listening to what is in their hearts and the difficulties they experience in ministry, one becomes aware of the personal experience that sustains the ordained ministry. And this is good for the priests, but it is also good for the bishop because it sharpens his ability to be a pastor, father, and brother for his lay brothers and sisters as well. It is also worth emphasizing that it is always in everyday life that this fraternity and fatherhood must be realized, so that it does not remain just a nice theory or a pious intention. For example, I remember that a training program was the opportunity to live together with a variety of priests, sharing different environments, from the kitchen to the chapel, and different moments of the day. Living this day-to-day is tiring, but it is a human and spiritual exercise of great importance for learning every day with and from others, thus becoming people capable of relationships. The real presence of the other, not just occasionally but in the form of a true sharing of life, challenges our selfishness and closure, our patience, our mutual tolerance of defects, until we open ourselves to welcoming the other and loving him or her.

The Bishop's Closeness

The relationship of personal closeness with priests, then, is obviously aimed at the pastoral service one is called to offer to the local Church. This is not a way of just getting along and surviving without conflict, but it is that human and spiritual basis necessary so that the pastoral orientations of a diocese can then be thought of together. The bishop is father and brother of priests, not because of a clerical choice that locks the presbytery into its own little world, but, on the contrary, in order to walk together with them in the service of the diocese and thus to initiate together with them the fundamental guidelines of the diocesan path. The ultimate goal of everything, of our personal life as a priest or bishop of a diocese, is always evangelization. This aspect is also necessary and indispensable: One cannot be a bishop alone, thinking of oneself as a leader at someone's command. One is always a bishop with the priests and with the people of God, with the priests and together with them in service to the people of God. Today, I believe this is a great challenge, a reality that is not easy and yet very important. We are faced with a fragmented, pluralistic society, often marked by a multiplicity of life experiences and values. Therefore, pastoral care must also be rich and diverse. It can only be thought of together, listening and dialoging, praying, and seeking ways together: bishops, priests, and laity. The keyword is "together."

To this we can add another important challenge, which is to try to liberate the episcopal ministry from an aura of sacredness and excessive institutional formality, which often offers a partial and misplaced image of the bishop. In some places, the bishop is still a personality, perhaps no longer feared but still revered. People do not always feel close to their bishop as a pastor, but they stop at his institutional role and often see him simply as "the authority" who decides matters.

We have to avoid falling into bureaucracy and functionalism. A bishop, as much as he can and in the forms he can, should be close to the people, listen to the pastoral workers, meet people—dare I say it—with normality and having simple human relationships.

The Call to Govern

Of course—and this is a permanent challenge that should not be taken for granted—the bishop is called to governance. Fraternity with the priests and laity and the exercise of spiritual paternity should not exempt the bishop from the call he has been given to be the one who leads, with charity and prophecy, the people of God. That never means to be authoritarian or simply a decision maker, but to take responsibility for the spiritual and pastoral life of the local Church. Thus he will be able to read situations, interpret them in the light of the possible good for that person and for the whole diocese, to deal with the thorniest cases and, without running away from them, to also have the courage to make choices. There are many moments in a bishop's life when he finds himself alone and vulnerable in front of complex issues, which may affect people or pastoral realities. While suffering, he must have the courage to make difficult and at times even radical decisions. The people also walk and grow thanks to the authority of a father who is loving and, out of love, instructs, admonishes, and offers guidance.

Looking at the episcopal ministry of the future, finally, I imagine that we need to commit to doing much more to overcome clericalism, which, behind the role being played, always results in a form of detachment from the people of God and in authoritarianism. Yet more work needs to be done to give an adequate form to the episcopal ministry in a context such as today's, characterized by constant change and by marked diversity. We cannot remain in a pastoral ministry of preservation. It takes the courage of a missionary pastoral ministry, concerned with meeting the people of our time with the joy of the Gospel. And this requires bishops capable of truly sharing in diocesan life, of immersing themselves in the pastoral work of Christian communities, together with priests and laity, maturing prophetic visions without merely preserving the existing state of things.

The Church Today
Ten Open Questions

The personal history of the Lord's disciple is also always an ecclesial history. Those who have received the anointing of the Spirit are taken into the great river of the Christian community, with its rich tradition and the varied forms that faith has taken over the centuries. They experience the encounter with God in a personal, but not in a private or individualistic way. Thus, they embrace the faith and accept the Word of the Gospel, walking together with their brothers and sisters in faith and, with them, facing the multiple challenges of the present time, without fear and with the ardor of one who desires to communicate the Good News to the world. It is important, therefore, for each Christian to come out of individualism and a faith reduced to personal sentiment or private consolation, feeling instead part of the Church and carrying out with the Church the dream of evangelization. In this regard, the words that Pope Francis wrote in Evangelii gaudium, remain fundamental, telling us that the Church is the first beneficiary of God's initiative of love and, therefore, she too must learn to always take the first step toward humanity, especially toward those who are far away: "An evangelizing community knows that the Lord has taken the initiative, he has loved us first (cf. 1 Jn 4:19), and therefore we can move forward, boldly take the initiative, go out to others, seek those who have fallen away, stand at the crossroads and welcome the outcast. Such a community has an endless desire to show mercy, the fruit of its own experience of the power of the Father's infinite mercy. Let us try a little harder to take the first step and to become involved" (EG 24). To go out, to seek the distant, to dare *to take the initiative, to involve oneself: These "moving" verbs, if we do not want them to remain empty slogans, imply the courage of reflection on some "hot" issues, from which Cardinal Lazarus did not shy away.*

⌒

Your Eminence, what do you think the Church is called to today, and what are the main challenges of evangelization, in a time like ours marked by indifference to the question of God?

Faced with this question, before any theoretical reflection, the image that instinctively comes to mind is that of some European bishops whom I have been meeting from time to time, since I have been Prefect of this Dicastery. Listening to them, I perceive their concern and suffering about how, in their countries, Christianity is losing attraction, the number of the faithful, and especially of priestly vocations, is decreasing, and they find themselves in a condition of minority and difficulty. Let us also say that, despite many analyses concerning this issue, there are no easy answers or recipes, and this is good. In fact, we are called to rediscover the vigor and enthusiasm for a new proclamation of the Gospel, as has been done since the beginnings of Christianity, when even then the outward social and cultural context was not at all conducive to the spread of the faith. Recently, Pope Francis gave us a text on Curia reform that begins, "*Praedicate evangelium* [preach the gospel] (cf. Mk 16:15; Mt 10:7-8). This is the task that the Lord Jesus entrusted to his disciples." I like to pair this with the evangelization that happens when we live charity because the Gospel is proclaimed not only with preaching made up of words, but with a life that radiates something beautiful and important, through gestures of closeness, of compassion, of love, that give a glimpse of the face of God and the beauty of his call. If we look at the primitive community in Jerusalem, we note the three main pillars: They live the Word. They put everything in common. They support those who are in difficulty, and therefore the poorest. For me, the challenge of evangelization is always first and foremost to be a Church that returns to proclaiming the Word, because the Word makes us discover and feel like brothers and sisters, and makes us no longer prioritize material goods or other external things, but love. Then, we open ourselves to sharing and charity toward those in need. In this regard, we also need a bit of self-criticism: Sometimes the salt has lost its flavor. Our Christianity risks being insipid, presenting itself as a set of rules or letting external and organizational aspects prevail. Instead, the Gospel must be at the center. It must be proclaimed anew and in a fresher way. And it must become lived charity.

⌒

Young people, especially, are far from the faith and Church life. Why do they not find a taste for the Gospel and reject the Church?

We need to listen to the youth universe. Sometimes, when we discuss the different categories of people, such as young people, families, or others, I have the impression that we have in our minds a theoretical definition of these people or an image and model that actually exists almost exclusively in our minds. The question is: Do we really know the way young people feel, think, and approach life today?

I think young people today are, first and foremost, thirsty for meaningful examples. They do not believe sermons; they distrust those who impose themselves on their vision of freedom in the name of some authority, but they open up, make themselves generously available, and let themselves be touched when they encounter witnesses of beauty and authenticity. They also need the religious question to be posed to them, no longer in the classical terms of an informative catechism or morality, but in the form of radical questions that can really interest them: How are you living? What do you want to do with your life? Think of how many people speak in this way in so many parts of the world, including through religious leaders, but especially through the voices of singers and other musicians, who draw huge crowds, sometimes conveying messages that have substance, that make people think, that speak to the feelings, emotions, pain, and hopes of young people. Do we, when we proclaim the Gospel, speak like this? This, of course, implies a renewal of our approaches and language. But I repeat: It cannot be done if we do not first listen to the world of youth, their troubles, and their criticisms, even going to where the young people are and where they live. Listening also teaches us the language with which to speak because listening is stripping oneself bare, creating an open space for the other. It is already an initial form of relationship.

~

Listening to one another and then walking together. This obviously brings out the theme of the Synod. But where are we with listening to the laity and their involvement? Where are we today with the role of the laity in the Church and with a vision of pastoral ministry, in which everyone has their own space and can offer their own charism?

Let's start by saying that the Synod is not just "something," but it is the style of the Church. For there to be Church, it is necessary to walk together, to listen together to the Word, to discern together our Christian witness in the world. And it is also a bit paradoxical that for many years we have been talking about "space for the laity," as if it were some kind of exception. In reality, the Church is the community of the baptized; that is, of the laity! For me, beyond theological clarifications, it is quite natural to think this way because the Church in Korea was born of the laity. Ours is the story of those who were surprised by the proclamation of the Gospel, read the books of Matteo Ricci, converted, and were baptized. And gradually, like those who really enter a world hitherto unknown, they discovered the importance and centrality of the weekly Christian rhythm, with the Sunday Eucharistic celebration. And then, from the community itself, they chose someone who would become a priest and celebrate for them, and then someone for the episcopate and so on. Just as it happened in the first apostolic community. It is Baptism that is the foundation of Christian life, the reality that unites us to the life of Christ and makes us witnesses of the Gospel in life. The forms and modalities of our witness, then, change according to the specific vocation we receive, lay people and priests. This must become a given because it is an original given of the Church. Today, I think the decline in vocations is in a providential way speeding up the process of greater involvement of the laity in the ecclesial mission, which should have happened naturally. We understand more and more that the priest cannot do everything, but we must learn to believe that he is not called to everything. And I think we need to equip ourselves and prepare ourselves more and more, within the Church, to form Christian leaders. We should not be afraid of this: Let's form real leaders, believers supported by solid spiritual, theological, and pastoral formation, who can flank priests and carry out the evangelical mission together with them, in the Church and the world. Without waiting for a shortage of priests to do this, let's start. Let's think about it. Let's select people willing to do this, and let's start preparing them for the future. In Asia, there are many such lay people, and the priests have many collaborators. This could be a concrete outcome of the synod process. To use an image: not the priest elevated, at the top of a ladder, but the priest who, with others, stands in a circle because in the center is Jesus.

‿

Obviously speaking of the laity, we cannot keep silent about the women's issue. What further reflection do we need to make on the role of women in the Church?

Sometimes we still give the impression of a macho world, especially in comparison to the path that has been taken in our societies on this issue. There are different levels to this issue because there is a theological-canonical level that concerns the fact of the roles of responsibility often too exclusively linked to the ministry of the Order, and, at the same time, there is a more general and pastoral level that concerns the simple and normal involvement of women in the life of the Church, often in roles and services that, in fact, they have already been fulfilling for centuries and that do not find formal recognition. From this point of view, Pope Francis has really been pushing us forward, and by also instituting women readers and acolytes, he has made a gesture of considerable importance. The Church has a female face. The best thing, in fact, so that it does not become just an issue relegated to discussions, conferences, and proclamations, is to make concrete gestures: to make female readers, to make acolytes, to involve women more and more in certain areas and in certain roles of government. Personally, I repeat: A woman is essential even in seminary formation teams, where precisely an exclusively male world generates quite a few problems. Let's move forward on this!

Your Eminence, let's also say a word about the scourge of clergy abuse and those ambiguous situations, especially related to the use of money, that perhaps call us to intervene in the formation of future priests. What to do?

Dealing with this area requires not only delicacy but also some preparation. We cannot be crude and dismiss problems by stopping at the surface. Often, in fact, a sexual issue is a symptom of something else, just as behind the attachment to money lie issues of a different nature and not just the fact itself. Certainly, the scourge of abuse is something dramatic, upsetting. To be honest, for this I suffer much, and I try to pray a lot. A great deal of work certainly needs to be done on the formation of future priests: first of all, to break down the clerical vision from which often derives that form of authoritarianism and moral abuse that then generates all the rest; to teach them to have a healthy relationship with their own bodies and their own sexuality; and for barriers and taboos to be broken down in the relationship with the opposite sex. In this context also falls the issue of money, which can be a surrogate, a need for security, or a means of self-aggrandizement. We need to form people who are free, serene, and detached. And we need to focus on ongoing formation for priests. Given a certain anthropological fragility, which is ours and from which we come because of so many troubled family situations, it is necessary not to lower our guard. We are always on the way. I am concerned when I see seminarians who, right from the start, seem to already know everything and are ready-made priests. In reality, until the last day of life, we are in need of something to learn, and therefore seminaries should not be factories for producing priests who are already perfect, but places that form people who are on a continuous journey of human growth and spiritual conversion.

You were chairman of the Peace Committee of the Bishops' Conference in Korea. What contribution can we give to build the universal brotherhood that Pope Francis often calls us to?

Korean history is strongly affected by divisions and the difficult relationship between the North and the South. As chairman of the Peace Committee, I have tried to take an interest in certain social issues. The Gospel is not an abstract theory, and Christian spiritual life is not a mysticism detached from the earth. On the contrary, when Jesus proclaims the face of the merciful God by healing the sick and forgiving sinners, he also causes a shake-up in the society of the time and in the political and religious power system that excluded the weakest. The first contribution we can make in this regard is frankness of speech, parrhesia, and prophecy. We must say out loud what is wrong, call evil by name, denounce the horrors of all violence and war, and defend the weak. The Church offers, in this regard, a contribution that is never directly political but represents a warning to society and to the conscience of individuals. For some, by taking a stand, I have become a "red bishop," but this cannot be taken seriously. It is the way through which those who feel disturbed by evangelical stances try to neutralize them. We should not be afraid to get our hands dirty for fear of having "enemies." More important than not having "enemies" is to make an examination of conscience every night and ask ourselves: How much have I contributed today to brotherhood, to peace, to spreading the commandment of love?

But what are the relations with North Korea today?

They are still very difficult on both sides. The 38th parallel, which is somewhat the demarcation line separating North and South, is apparently recognized by both sides, but a certain tension runs beneath the surface. In such cases, dialogue is difficult because a strongly ideological view is ingrained, according to which people are divided into left and right.

〜

What contribution can the Asian Church make to our weary West, which has long been experiencing a deep spiritual and ecclesial crisis?

A certain secularism that pervades not only society but also the very vision of personal life is now widespread everywhere. Asian society also has its own problems and its rich diversity; we are talking about a highly multicultural, multireligious, modern, and globalized continent. However, the desire for God is rooted in Asian people; the demand for spirituality is grafted into them as their constitutive trait. The Church has so far been able to be an interpreter of this demand, not to suppress it with a negative proclamation, but to present the Gospel through the principal symbols of life and a witness of spirituality and joy. The way is always this:

the encounter between faith and culture. In the West, Christianity perhaps needs new readings of reality and people's lives to reformulate the question about God in a new way.

〜

What word would you like to address today to priests around the world?

I would like priests to be conscious of the greatness of their calling. Not a greatness that makes them proud or feel different and superior, but, on the contrary, that should make them grateful, open, and living in a continuous "surprise." In most seminaries around the world, there is a painting of Jesus washing the disciples' feet. This means that Jesus takes off his outer garments, puts on an apron, and descends; he lowers himself. I would like to say to priests today: Know how to live the ministry by becoming like the Good Samaritan; know how to go down into concrete life, stoop to the wounds, and wash the feet of humanity. Know how to be men of dialogue and communion.

〜

What do the figure and magisterium of the late Pope Francis represent for today's world?

On the figure of Pope Francis, whatever is said risks being too little. We were before a presence of spirit embodied in a rich humanity that expressed closeness and compassion. But there was one thing about Pope Francis that always attracted and moved me: He was great because he was attentive to small things! He was attentive to details, to people, to stories. I cannot forget his visit to Asia, when he met a Buddhist security worker who was unable to have children. The Pope told him he would pray for him. When I came to Rome, after some time, and had an audience, [Pope Francis] asked me about that person, even remembering his last name. I was able to relate this to the man, who remained very amazed and happy. In time, he became a Catholic, and he and his wife decided to adopt a little girl. I baptized her, and then I invited them to Rome to greet the Holy Father. This, I think, was the real greatness of Pope Francis, and it says something important about the Gospel and faith: God is near; he remembers us; he takes care even of the details of our lives. This is the essence of the Christian faith. And we had the grace of a pope who always reminded us of it.

Conclusion

In his message for the 54th World Communications Day, celebrated on January 24, 2020, Pope Francis wished to emphasize the importance of storytelling; that is, the art of narrating so as to grasp and breathe the truth and beauty of good stories, which build up rather than destroy. Even Jesus, says Pope Francis, spoke to us about God and his plan of love, not with abstract speeches but with parables—short narratives, taken from everyday life. Here, life becomes a story, and then, for the listener, the story becomes life. That narrative enters the life of the listener and transforms it.

Thus, inserted into the great stream of salvation history, which has been told and handed down to us, we too can discover that every person is a story to be told, a treasure chest in which past and present are preserved, a tile that makes up the mosaic of the world, a great open book whose pages are to be explored with wonder. When we tell someone's story and give voice to his or her voice, we are becoming weavers of the future. Indeed, a unique, original, and inescapable richness emerges from each story that helps us interpret life's journey and opens up new and unexpected paths.

This is the grateful memory I keep in my heart after meeting weekly with Cardinal Lazarus You Heung-sik. The feeling of inner gratitude for his kindness, his smile, and his exquisite humanity is combined with the awareness of having found myself before the beauty of a true, authentic story, narrated with simplicity, which unfolded before me like a gift of precious evangelical, spiritual, and pastoral insights for the Church of the future.

I sincerely hope that the reader can also be touched by the warmth of the sun that, "like the lightning" that "comes from the East and *shines as far as the West" (Mt 24:27), rises from these pages to warm the heart and illuminate the path.*

Francesco Cosentino

FOCOLARE MEDIA

Enkindling the Spirit of Unity

The New City Press book you are holding in your hands is one of the many resources produced by Focolare Media, which is a ministry of the Focolare Movement in North America. The Focolare is a worldwide community of people who feel called to bring about the realization of Jesus' prayer: "That all may be one" (see John 17:21).

Focolare Media wants to be your primary resource for connecting with people, ideas, and practices that build unity. Our mission is to provide content that empowers people to grow spiritually, improve relationships, engage in dialogue, and foster collaboration within the Church and throughout society.

Visit www.focolaremedia.com to learn more about all of New City Press's books, our award-winning magazine *Living City*, videos, podcasts, events, and free resources.

NCP
NEW CITY PRESS

www.ingramcontent.com/pod-product-compliance
Lightning Source LLC
LaVergne TN
LVHW021523080426
835509LV00018B/2622